REAL
ADVICE

from
"The Real Estate Advisors"

50 of Your Real Estate and Investing Questions Answered

Cindy Cooper

Parker House Publishing

ParkerHouseBooks.com
Printed in the United States of America

A compilation of radio show segments
as heard on WFSU-FM and Florida Public Radio in
Tallahassee, Florida, and the surrounding counties.

Introduction

Cindy Cooper is a top-selling real estate agent in Tallahassee, Florida and the surrounding areas, and has been for more than 35 years. She is "The Real Estate Advisors" heard on WFSU-FM, on Florida Public Radio. The Real Estate Advisors airs once a week to answer questions and give great advice on all aspects of real estate — from owning to financing to fixing up.

This book is a compilation of the scripts from those shows that have aired over the years. Some chapters are a little longer than the original airing, as I was thrilled to be able to expand just a few that really needed a little more information, but had to be cut and edited to fit the time parameters of the show.

Real estate selling and buying comes with probably more than its fair share of stories, facts, and fictions. These chapters cover the facts and fiction. The stories, well, that is for another book...

If you would like to listen to the shows this book was based on, visit www.TLHRealtors.com and enjoy the podcasts.

Table of Contents

I. Top Questions, Plus Ideas to Make Your Home Look Fabulous!

How is the market doing? 3

What are the top questions that buyers ask sellers?.................. 5

What are the best improvements to do now that will help improve the resale value of my home later? 7

Which home improvements recoup the most money?.............. 9

What are the new trends to look for in homes today?............. 11

What features are most wanted by homeowners? 13

Could it be my home is outdated?... 15

What should I do inside my house to stage it for a showing?... 17

What can we do to increase our curb appeal? 19

What maintenance should I be doing?.................................... 21

How can I save money on plumbing repairs? 23

What can I do to build the perfect patio?................................. 25

I am buying a house that has polybutylene pipes. Should I be concerned?.. 27

How can I keep my home safer from burglars?......................... 29

II. Money, Mortgages and Scams

How do I check my credit report and score? 33

How much money do I need to buy a house? 35

How much house can I buy? 37

Should I buy or rent? 39

Am I ready to buy a home? 41

I am going to buy a house — what can I do to ensure a
smooth and easy closing? 43

Do you have any good negotiation tips to share? 45

What are these new closing disclosures? 47

Why do deals fall apart? 49

What exactly is title insurance? 51

I am hearing a lot about wire fraud in closings. What
should I watch for? 53

Should I save my money or buy investment property for
retirement? 55

Should I sell or rent my current house? 57

Is Real Estate a good investment? (Yes, but so is
compound interest) 59

I am looking to buy an auction property. What should I
do? 61

What is the difference between a foreclosure and a short sale?... 63

Why do short sales take so long? 65

I found a great rental online, but they want me to mail the deposit out of the country — is this a scam?...................... 67

How do I protect my property listing from rental scams?..... 69

I am looking at my tax roll assessment, is that what my house is really worth? 71

What is the Save Our Homes Amendment? 73

III. Home Selling To Home Buying, Moving And Miscellaneous

When is the buying season for houses?......................... 77

Is there ever a time or a market when nothing sells?............. 79

I've bought a house — what type of inspections do I need? 81

I am a For Sale By Owner — any advice on showing my home?... 83

When a buyer is coming to look at my home, should I be there for the showing? 85

What is the difference between 'as-is' compared to 'warranted?' 87

What is the difference between a warranted home and a home warranty?.. 89

I am moving — do I have to move everything? 91

What are some good tips for moving?................................. 93

Do you have any ideas to make moving easier? 95

How can I find a good repair guy? 97

How do I become a real estate agent? 99

What is the oldest building in Tallahassee? 101

Conclusion...103

I.
Top Questions, Plus Ideas to Make Your Home Look Fabulous!

How is the market doing?

This is always one of the first questions I am asked. The Tallahassee market is rebounding nicely. Most of Tallahassee has hit the bottom already and is working its way back up. There are many neighborhoods in town that have not had any foreclosure activity in the last few years and have stabilized back to a normal market. The prices are increasing about 2 to 3% a year, which is what the market was doing before the crash, and that is very sustainable appreciation.

The main problem area now is the NW. With all the new construction around the university that can house an additional 8000 people and only 300 new students a year to take up those spaces, they are pulling renters and buyers from the surrounding neighborhoods, putting downward pressure on prices and rents in those areas.

2-3 percent a year growth

So, if there are still six foreclosures on a street, that neighborhood has still not seen the bottom yet, although this does lead to some incredible bargains in those neighborhoods now.

What are the top questions that buyers ask sellers?

When a buyer finally finds the home of their dreams, they often have a list of questions for the seller. There are, however, certain questions that come up time and time again. If you are looking to sell your home, take the time to answer some of these questions and leave a seller's disclosure, or other information at the house, so the buyers will see it when they are there looking at your home. It is helpful to leave out a notebook with information for the buyers to flip through. Have extra copies of your disclosure available that they can take with them.

The most frequently asked questions are:

- How old is the house?

- When was it last renovated? Be sure to include all the details of your work here.

- Who did the work and were all the appropriate permits pulled? (It would not hurt to leave the receipts and permits in your notebook)

- How old is the roof?
- What appliances and fixtures are included in the sale?
- How much are the homeowner association fees, average utility bills, lawn service, or pool maintenance? Put a bill from each in your notebook for the buyer to see.
- How old is the air conditioner unit? When was it last serviced?

Sellers who provide the answers to these questions before they are asked will save time, and appear to be very helpful and honest to the buyer.

What are the best improvements to do now that will help improve the resale value of my home later?

If you are looking to sell your home in a few years, you don't want to pay for impractical or expensive improvements now that will be out of style by the time you put a for sale sign in the yard. You want to look at traditional and fashionable upgrades that will provide value and aesthetic beauty for years to come.

New kitchens top the list, and at least new countertops and appliances are usually a sure bet. Bathrooms are next — be sure to avoid all white as that usually looks too sterile. Bring in some light by adding skylights or sun tunnels if you can. Put up some extra storage shelves or cabinets to reduce the clutter in your home.

Add an island into the kitchen. Put down hardwood floors. There are some great new tile options also. If you are thinking of new carpet that may need to be redone again before you put your home up for sale. Popular outdoor items include fireplaces, decks, patios, fountains, and landscaping. And an outdoor kitchen will always boost the wow factor for your resale.

Which home improvements recoup the most money?

The new yearly cost vs. value report is out and the number one project for return on your investment is.... attic insulation, with an average return of over 107%! Now, this is not a high-cost project, so, let's take a look at some others.

———

Home improvement can be projects that upgrade an existing home interior, exterior, or other improvements to the property (i.e. garden work or garage)

———

If you are doing a major kitchen or bathroom remodel — the average return is 50 to 60% of your investment dollars. But if you are looking at just a minor remodel, those numbers jump to 60 to 80%.

Next with a high return is a front door replacement in the 70 to 90% range. Depending on if you are doing just the door or the whole entrance, and also if you are using a regular door or a steel door. This is followed by a garage door replacement in the 75 to 80% range.

Window replacements will get you 70 to 75% of your money back, and generators and decks will give you a solid 50 to 60 percent return on your money.

What are the new trends to look for in homes today?

The next big trend I see coming up is home automation. People want to control more and more aspects of their homes through their smartphones. Smart home technologies will add utility as well as value to your home, as some buyers are now looking for these features to already be in place when they buy a home. You can probably get a starter kit of smart devices to enhance your home for about $1000. There are 3 basic technologies to look for.

- The first is Home Systems control. That would regulate your temperature and lighting control, and turn the appliances on and off when you are not home.

- Next, you would have Home Accessibility Products that can allow a homeowner to grant access to their home remotely or open and close the garage door.

- And lastly, you want to look for security and monitoring products that can monitor your home remotely and send you notifications in case of any disturbance.

What features are most wanted by homeowners?

I was reading an interesting article the other day on the top 13 features that homeowners want the most. Surprisingly, the number one item was a laundry room. By a whopping 92%. So when people ask me for advice on what upgrades to look at, or where to concentrate their limited renovation budget or what type of things to consider adding to their floor plan when building a new home, these are the features I think they should keep in mind.

92

percent laundry room

The number one thing — is a laundry room. This is followed by energy star appliances, then exterior lighting, next is a larger kitchen and bathrooms. No real surprise there. Number 5 is energy star windows. That is followed by ceiling fans at number 6. Next on the list is a patio. Number 8 is a full bathroom on the main level. Number 9, hardwood floors. Number 10, more insulation.

Next up is garage storage, followed by an eat-in kitchen. And coming in at number 13 is a walk-in pantry.

Could it be my home is outdated?

If you are thinking of putting your house on the market soon, it is time to take a step back and take a cold hard look at your décor. You may still love some of the dated touches you have put in years ago, or maybe you don't want to go through the trouble and expense of updating to current colors and finishes. I do understand, but once you put your house on the market, it is no longer your house anymore, and you need to start looking at it from a potential buyer's point of view.

The things that scream "dated" the most to buyers are:

- White appliances

- Busy wallpaper and bold paint colors.

- Dated fixtures and hardware — especially anything with a gold finish. Take a good look at your lighting, ceiling fans, knobs, hinges, vents, and grates. Also, consider your front door hardware and kick plate.

- Tile countertops
- Popcorn ceilings
- Carpet in the bathrooms
- Shag carpet anywhere
- Wood paneling
- Linoleum floors

Choose materials and colors that are neutral and will appeal to a wide range of people. Aiming for neutrality is the best way to ensure your home is in fashion, and will not turn off any buyers.

What should I do inside my house to stage it for a showing?

If you are looking to make a good first impression on a buyer when your house is being shown, a little work upfront will go a long way. First and foremost, you need to clear off the clutter from all surfaces. You want your home to show like a model home. No surface should have more than 3 items on it and the bigger the items are, the better.

You don't have to clear out an entire closet to make it feel bigger, but clear enough out so that 1/3 of it is empty.

Also, any bookcases and pantries should have a few shelves that are 1/3 empty. Take down your personal pictures. Do a thorough cleaning of the entire house and pay extra attention to the kitchen and bathrooms, as these rooms must be spotless. Have your tile and grout steam cleaned by a carpet cleaner. They will look brand new.

———————

"It doesn't hurt to bake some cookies."

———————

What can we do to increase our curb appeal?

Curb appeal is very important. It often makes the difference between someone deciding to look at your home or not. Stand across the street and take an honest appraisal of what a potential buyer will see. Make sure all the beds are weeded and new pine straw or pine bark is put down. Add some flowers to give it a splash of color.

When was the last time you used your front door? Polish up the hardware and paint the door. Better yet, replace the hardware and add a new kick plate. Make sure the glass is sparkling clean. Brush away all the spider webs. Pressure wash the front steps, walkways, driveway and parking areas.

What about your mailbox? Give it a fresh coat of paint and replace the numbers. If someone is driving along looking for the address, this is the first thing that will catch their eye.

A little bit of effort and a modest budget can make a big difference in your homes curb appeal. Set the tone right and get ready to invite buyers inside your home.

What maintenance should I be doing?

It is always a good idea to keep up on the maintenance at your home, whether you are thinking of selling or not. Have your heat and air conditioner serviced once a year and replace the air filter every 3 months.

Keeping bugs out can be as simple as repairing holes in window and door screens. You can also keep bugs out by sealing cracks and holes on the outside of the house, think of any faucets or pipes that are protruding from the wall.

On the inside, seal baseboards, behind the sinks, and around the pipes and windows. Speaking of windows, make sure yours are in good condition and have a tight fit. Clean the tracks and replace any torn or missing weather stripping. Preventing outside air from leaking in will help to reduce your energy bills.

Clean your gutter of debris. This will keep them working and help to avoid any woodrot that occurs from water overflow. Focusing on these small jobs now can lead to big savings of your time and money in the future.

Focusing on these small jobs now can lead to big savings of your time and money in the future.

How can I save money on plumbing repairs?

Every home has plumbing issues at some point. One of the best ways to save money on plumbing repairs is usually old fashioned preventative maintenance, most of which you can do yourself.

In order to fix leaks timely, you have to be able to see them. Don't treat that space under your sink as a storage cabinet, treat it like maintenance space. Keep it clean and clear.

Your garbage disposal is not a trash can — keep the grease out and run hot water through it during and after use. Throw some ice in occasionally and run to sharpen the blades.

It is not normal for your sink to take 10 minutes to drain. Use a drain cleaner or clean out the p-trap underneath the sink.

Dripping faucets and running toilets are usually in the realm of most do-it-yourselfers. The parts are cheap and you can find manuals and tutorials online to guide you.

These are the easy fixes, but if the problem goes beyond these, it may be time to call in a professional.

What can I do to build the perfect patio?

Patios are great and can be enjoyed almost year-round here. The first thing to consider when you are putting in a patio is just like any other real estate — location, location, location.

How are you going to use your patio? Do you want every minute in the sun or a little shelter in the shade? Do you want the patio near the house for easy access, or maybe down in a flat spot if you have a sloping yard, or near a tranquil spot?

Next, think of the size and shape you want for your patio. Also think of adding built-ins such as seating, fire pits, planters, water features, maybe even a hot tub! Do you want space for an outdoor kitchen or grill to be added later on?

Laying pipes and stubbing out for future use is easy to do now.

Materials vary widely — the concrete patios of today can be tinted, dyed, stamped and decorated in many different ways.

There is also natural stone, flagstone, clay bricks, and pavers that come in a variety of shapes, sizes, and colors.

Make sure you check on the location of any utility cables before you start digging.

I am buying a house that has polybutylene pipes. Should I be concerned?

Polybutylene is a form of plastic that was used extensively for water supply piping from 1978 to 1995 as a cheap substitute for copper pipes. They are usually grey, but they can be white with a dull finish.

There are several different kinds of polybutylene pipes, but there is one in particular that has the wrong type of fittings. These are the ones that cause most of the problems. The pipes themselves are OK, but the fittings tend to break, crack or fail in some way and cause water leaks.

Your home inspector should check for these pipes in your home inspection.

You will also want to check with your insurance company for their policy on coverage for these pipes if you have them. Some insurance companies will say they cover the pipes, but then they will exclude water damage, which is the type of damage you will have, so they are not really covering your polybutylene pipes.

If you do find you have polybutylene pipes, you have the option of changing out the pipes to copper for usually a couple of thousand dollars. If this is a new discovery to the seller, sometimes they will cover or split the cost of replacement with you.

How can I keep my home safer from burglars?

By now everyone knows not to put the box from your new TV out on the street. It just screams "Come and get me!" to any potential burglars.

Some other good ideas are to maintain the outside of your property. Not only will it look good and keep your neighbors happy, but a well-maintained yard deters thieves and vandals who target vacant houses.

Know your neighbors. Introduce them to your real estate agent, so they know who will be coming and going from your home.

Embrace the power of lighting. Have security lights and bright lights in front of your house and in back. Lock your doors, and reinforce those locks. Invest in good locks and strike plates and a solid door frame. Even that old fashioned timing device to turn on and off lamps is still a good idea.

And, don't forget new technology. Not only do most new buyers ask for it, but it can also make your home safety a snap.

Smart home technology can remotely control lighting and music, see who is at your front door, and even change the thermostat. There are new security systems that can monitor your home and send you a notice if there are any disturbances.

II
Money, Mortgages and Scams

How do I check my credit report and score?

Checking your credit report at least once a year or even more is imperative in this day and age of cybercrime and information hacking. People's identities and even business identities are stolen every day. One of the best things you can do is check through your entire credit report once a year, even if you have had no problems that you are aware of. The  government has a site that you can check once a year, that will not cost you any money, and will not count as an inquiry on your credit report.

You can access a copy of your credit report from all three credit reporting agencies by visiting www.annualcreditreport.com. Obtaining your actual credit score on this site may require payment of a nominal fee, but the credit report itself is free of charge, and this is the most important part to look over.

Other sites advertised are commercial sites and will charge a fee to access your credit report and will show up as an inquiry on your credit report, which may lower your score.

How much money do I need to buy a house?

Closing costs are always a big question on every home buyer's mind. There are 3 main parts to closing costs.

- First is the down payment. That is the amount you put down for your mortgage. This is between you and your bank, anywhere from 3% to 5% or even up to 25% or more depending on the program and loan you are using. If you are going for a VA loan, you would have a zero down payment option.

- Then you have "the" closing costs such as title insurance, appraisal, survey, documentary stamp fees, bank underwriting fees — that sort of thing. Those usually run about 3% of the sales price.

- And finally, you have the prepaid costs, which is setting up an escrow account to pay for your taxes and insurance.

Not mentioned here, but important to consider, is don't forget your inspection fees and moving expenses.

If you are buying a house for $200,000, and putting down 5% with the bank, your costs are going to run about $19,000. That is the amount of money you would need to bring to closing. The 5% down payment will be $10,000 of it. Then there is about $6000 in closing costs and another $3000 for pre-paids. But, in many cases, you can ask the seller to pay some of your closing costs.

You always have to pay your own down payment and prepaids, but you can negotiate with the seller to pay most or part of your closing costs, usually up to 3%. In this case, if the seller paid 3% of your closing costs it would save you $6000, so you would only have to bring $13,000 instead of $19,000 to closing.

How much house can I buy?

Knowing how much house you can buy at the beginning of your home search will save you a lot of grief down the road.

Your best bet to answering this question is to call a local bank or mortgage company. They can give you very accurate figures. They can also send you a prequalification letter, which you will need when you want to write a contract anyways.

But, if you are looking for a quick and dirty way to figure out what price range you can afford, start with your monthly gross salary. Take 28% to 32% of that depending on what type of loan you are getting. This is the maximum amount of monthly mortgage payment you can have.

Then take 43% of your monthly gross salary (what you make, not what you take home). This is the maximum amount of TOTAL monthly debt you can have, including your mortgage. Why just 43%?

Because they want you to have enough money left over to pay your income taxes, buy food, gas, have money to live on, etc. So, take that 43% amount and subtract your monthly payments like your car payment and credit cards (use only the minimum monthly payment due on your credit card for this figure) and the final figure is what you qualify for. Or the 28% figure, whichever is lower.

This will give you the monthly amount of a mortgage payment you can afford and still pay your other bills. Once you have the amount of monthly payment you can afford you can figure out the price range of house to look for.

Remember when you are figuring out your price range that your monthly payment is more than just the principal and interest. It will also include your property taxes and home insurance and possibly a mortgage interest amount. Add at least $250 to $300 a month, depending on your price range, to the monthly payment for your taxes and insurance.

Should I buy or rent?

I am often asked the question is it better to rent or buy a house?

Length of time is one of the biggest factors in making this decision. You need to ask yourself — How long do you plan on living in this area? Is your job stable? How long are you planning on working there? Are you subject to being transferred for your job? Do you have any looming family issues that may take you out of town for an extended period of time?

If you think you are likely to stay in the house for less than 1 to 3 years, then it is better to rent than buy. The market in most of Tallahassee is back to normal where you can make about 2 to 3 percent appreciation a year on your home. That means it will take you about 2 years just to be able to break even if you had to sell your home to move.

After 3 years you should see some equity again, and typically you can double your money in 10 to 12 years. But if you are going to be in your home for less than 3 years, you should look at renting.

Am I ready to buy a home?

If you are wondering if a home purchase is a good decision for you, here are a few questions to ask yourself.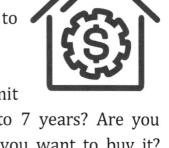

Do you have the desire to commit to the same community for 5 to 7 years? Are you stable in your career? Why do you want to buy it? Buying a home is a great way to increase your personal wealth. Most of the "old money" in this country was acquired through real estate investments.

Are your finances ready? Do you have good credit? Do you have a pattern of paying your bills on time? And, do you have any savings? If you are looking to buy a $200,000 home you need about $19,000 for a down payment, closing costs and prepaids. This is the amount you would need to bring to closing.

Then you have deposits to turn on utilities and cable services.

Don't forget about your moving expenses.

You should also have some cash reserves for any unexpected surprises that might come up. I had to put in a new sewer line and bring it around a big tree in an older home I recently bought. That took my entire landscaping and decorating budget plus a little bit more....

But, if you can answer yes to these questions, then a home purchase may be right for you!!

I am going to buy a house — what can I do to ensure a smooth and easy closing?

There are 3 main things you can do that will make your real estate closing as hassle-free as possible.

First — get preapproved for a loan. Have the bank or mortgage lender give you a prequalification letter. You will need this when you write a contract. Working with your lender ahead of time to secure your financing not only helps determine what you can afford, but it also helps uncover any problems that might come up and impact your closing.

Second — Listen to your lender and your Realtor. Buying a home involves a mountain of paperwork, so be prepared. And just when you think you are done submitting the last of the forms, the bank will undoubtedly want something more, sometimes even another copy of something you have already given them. Give it to them again. Always respond to your lender and Realtor requests very promptly.

And third — stay calm. Everyone agrees — Be flexible, be responsive, and above all, remain calm. Your lender will ask you for all kinds of last-minute details. Repairs will come up or not be done in a timely manner. Don't take it personally; sometimes things just come up at the last minute. Stay calm and keep your eye on the prize — closing on and owning your new home.

Do you have any good negotiation tips to share?

Yes, I do know a few. First off, always counter every contract and counter quickly. Don't let your potential buyers "cool down" or find another home while they are waiting for your reply. No one is still as excited about a deal 4 days later.

Next, send a clear signal that you are slowing down. You can do this by offering less and less each time you counter back. Start with changing your offer by $5000, then $3000, and your next offer by $1000.

If you want them to come down $5000 on their price, start at $10,000 off the asking price. You want to leave yourself enough room to go back and forth a couple of times.

Never start with your best or final offer, and never say during negotiations "this is my final offer." It is too hard to go back if you don't really mean that.

But, all that being said, if there is another offer on the table, then all negotiations go right out the window. You need to be prepared to offer full price or more if you have decided this is indeed your new home.

What are these new closing disclosures?

Since October 1st, 2015, new required closing disclosures went into effect. These are the statements that you receive at the closing that lists all of your closing costs and the amount of money you are bringing to the closing of your new home. The traditional good faith estimate, the truth in lending disclosure and the HUD-1 are all being combined and streamlined to provide consumers more transparency regarding what they are paying for a mortgage and the related closing costs.

You will now get a loan estimate at the beginning of your loan process and a closing disclosure at the end that is similar so you can easily compare what you were promised when you applied for your loan, and what you pay in closings costs at the closing table.

The new disclosure must be provided 3 days before closing. Check this disclosure thoroughly as soon as you get it, and call your lender immediately if you notice any problems. If the bank needs to make any adjustments, that triggers another 3 day period for the disclosures, which can delay your closing.

Why do deals fall apart?

Sometimes things don't go according to plan. Some of the main things that come up are:

First — Buyer's remorse. This sets in anywhere from an hour to a few days after the ink has dried on the contract. Everyone has second thoughts, but think long and hard about your end goal before doing anything permanent. I have had plenty of deals canceled due to temporary cold feet that buyers have begged me to put back together a week later. But it is usually too late by then.

Next up would be repairs. Anywhere from misunderstanding who will fix what to thinking a repair will be $10,000 when the reality is the figure is not even close to that. Real facts and figures help here. Get an estimate from one or two contractors and see what that repair really costs. What you thought was a $10,000 problem may actually be a surprisingly simple — and easy fix that will only cost $200 to $1000.

The third problem is — surprise! Buyers are sometimes not good money managers. This is not the time to take out any new debt or spend the money that the bank expects to be in your account. This is not the time for buying cars or that couch that will look great in your new living room. But you would be surprised by the number of people that do this.

And last, financing. Many times these days, even if they are prequalified, you don't really know if your buyer is actually going to get a loan until a few days before closing.

What exactly is title insurance?

Title insurance is an insurance policy that covers insuring the title to your home. If you bought a house and someone comes and knocks on your door and says, you know, an uncle of mine camped out here 40 years ago and owns part of this property.

That is where your title insurance would come in. They will go to court or they will fix the problem or they will pay you back for any losses that you might incur from such a claim.

The title company or attorney who does your closing will do a thorough title search for you, going back as much as 30 years to check for any claims, deed changes or judgments that aren't satisfied or taken care of. They will make sure there are no tax liens or mechanical and other liens on your house and check for any nasty surprises that sometimes come up during these searches.

At closing you will get clear title to your property,

so you don't have to worry about answering your door!

A title is the legal documentation that includes the specifics about the property you are purchasing and who owns it, often in the form of a deed.

I am hearing a lot about wire fraud in closings. What should I watch for?

One of the big problems today with closings is wire fraud. Crooks are getting very sophisticated in finding emails of people in real estate transactions and go to great lengths to recreate those email chains to look like you are getting new wire instructions from your lender or realtor.

You will open an email that says, the wiring instructions have been changed, please send your wire to dot dot dot.... It will look like it is from Cindy Cooper but the last name is spelled with an e instead of an r at the end, and the whole email chain that you have been a part of is there beneath it. It is very easy to miss.

Once the wire is sent, even if you catch it right away, usually the money is moved within minutes and is gone. The big key is to never trust wire instructions sent through email. Always call the source directly and verify all wiring information verbally.

The big key is to never trust wire instructions sent through email.

Should I save my money or buy investment property for retirement?

That is a good question. Let's look at some numbers. I talked with a good friend of mine who is a financial planner. I asked how much money would I have to save if I retired in 15 to 20 years and wanted to make $2000 a month from the money I had saved. She ran the numbers and came back to me and said I would have to save $800,000. Now, if I started a small savings/investment account when I was in my 20's, compound interest would have made up for a lot of that. But starting at 50, it is up to me and my savings.

So, I can save $800,000 in the next 15 to 20 years, or, I can find a property that costs $200,000 to $220,000 that makes about $2000 a month in rent. I could buy that investment property for a 25% down payment, which would be $50,000, plus another $6000 to $8000 in closing costs. The mortgage would be about $1100 a month on a 30 year fixed rate of 4.25%. That payment would include everything known as PITI (principal, interest, taxes, insurance) meaning the payment for principal and interest on the loan and about another $300 a month for the taxes and insurance escrow account. So, payment of $1100 to $1200 depending on your taxes and insurance. Barring having a lot of repairs to the property, you should be able to make about $10,000 a year. Send that $10,000, (or as much as you can), as an extra payment to your mortgage once a year and you should have the property paid off in 15 to 20 years. Then you would make the $2000 a month from the rent.

You can make payments more than once a year, there several different theories on that. But the important thing is to make the extra payments.

So, you can make $2000 a month for retirement in 15 to 20 years by either saving $800,000 or spending $50,000 now on an investment property.

Should I sell or rent my current house?

If you don't need the cash out of your current home to buy your next home and are prepared to be a landlord (and all that entails), a rental can provide predictable, long term income.

Your first consideration is can you afford 2 homes. You need to be able to qualify for the new home purchase and be able to pay all the costs for both properties, including mortgages payments, repairs, upkeep, yard maintenance, insurance, taxes, etc.

Next, consider if the old property is likely to appreciate. You can never predict the future, but you can determine if trends in your neighborhood are pointing toward up and coming or on the decline.

Also, you want to look at any tax consequences. If you have owned your home for a long period of time, you probably have a great amount of equity built up. You can write off capital gains on your homestead when you sell, but not after it has been turned into a long term rental property, so be sure you are not throwing away a significant tax write off. Check with your accountant on the current tax code for what you are planning to do.

Is Real Estate a good investment? (Yes, but so is compound interest)

Yes, real estate is almost always a good investment. Many people, including many old-money families, have made much of their wealth through real estate. But, if you are under the age of 25- there is another great investment to look into. It is the magic of compound interest.

If you could invest $5000 right now, at a reasonable rate of return, you should be able to double your money every 5 to 7 years. If you are under 25, you should be able to double that money 8 to 9 times. You would be in your 70's by then, but this will be a great addition to your portfolio of assets. And the easiest one!

Let's look at the numbers. Put away $5000 right now. It would next be $10,000 then $20,000, $40,000, $80,000, then $160,000, goes to $320,000, then $640,000 — Nice! Then $1.2 million dollars. The pop at the end really makes it worth it. $1.2

million dollars if you can put away $5000 right now and don't touch it until then.

If that seems out of reach, invest $100 right now. Everyone can come up with $100. Wash someone's car, save your birthday money, have a yard sale. Invest $100 today and it will be $100,000 when you are in your 70's. And it will be the easiest $100,000 you will ever make.

I am looking to buy an auction property. What should I do?

When an auction property comes up on the market over the internet, you can usually bid on it over a couple of days. But most of the action is going to happen in the last hour or two of the auction, and some bidding sites will extend the auction as long as people are still actively bidding on it. I usually suggest waiting at least until the last day to put in your first bid, so you don't run up the price any more than you have to.

If you win the auction, Congratulations! - You have just bought the house and have to be prepared to put down a deposit and buyer's premium immediately. Make sure you have done all of your homework and due diligence before now because it is very difficult and costly to back out at this point if they let you back out at all. Many auction companies will charge you a large chunk of change — over $15,000 — if you decide not to close on the house. There is no contingency period, you will be charged whether it is one minute after the auction or the day of closing.

Before you bid, make sure you have a thorough home inspection done along with a termite and woodrot inspection. Have your attorney or title company run a title search on the property to make sure there are no outstanding mechanical liens, tax or other liens, or other problems with the property history or title. There are usually repairs you will have to do, but auctions can be a great way to get a good price on the house.

What is the difference between a foreclosure and a short sale?

A foreclosure is a property that is wholly owned by the bank. They have gone through the entire process of obtaining the property back from the owner. They know what all the fees, payoffs and attorney costs are at this point because everything is done. The bank can negotiate with you, and can usually give you an answer on your offer within 48 hours and can close on the property in 30 to 60 days, or even sooner with a cash buyer. But they can actually set a closing date, whereas with a short sale the closing date is up in the air for quite some time.

A short sale is a property that still has the owner involved in the sale process. The owner is trying to sell the property for less than they owe on their mortgage. The seller has probably not made a payment on the property for at least 4 months because it takes that long before the bank will even consider talking to you about a short sale. So, your offer goes to the owner first. Once you have worked out a deal there, it goes to the bank. The bank sits on it for a while, or so it seems, then they go back and negotiate with the owner for whatever shortfall on the balance is still owned. Once that is worked out, the bank then comes back and gives you an answer on your offer. It often takes 2 to 6 months to hear back on your offer, (usually closer to 6 months or more), and then another 30 to 60 days to close depending on your financing. For a short sale, your timeline to close must be totally flexible and a ways out. It can run, if you are lucky and the seller and bank have gone through most of the process, anywhere from 2 months to a year to close on a short sale.

Foreclosures and short sales are often a great way to get a bargain on a home, depending, of course, on the work that is needed on the home.

Why do short sales take so long?

Despite the name short sale, there is nothing short or quick about a short sale. With a short sale, the owner of a property is trying to sell their property for less than they owe on their mortgage. When you put in an offer, you start with the owner. Once you have agreed upon a price with the property owner, the contract then goes to the bank. The bank figures out what is the least they can take on the mortgage, then they go back to the owner and negotiate with them whether the owner will pay the deficiency and how, or will the bank write off what is left on the mortgage.

Will it be reported to the credit bureaus, etc. Once all that is agreed upon, the bank replies back to the buyer with an acceptance or counter offer. This often takes about 2 to 6 months (usually closer to 6 months) just to hear back on your offer, and then it will take another 30 to 60 days to close.

There is nothing quick about a short sale, but for

those buyers that have the patience and no set timelines, they can be a chance to get an incredible bargain on a home.

———————————————

There is nothing quick about a short sale...

———————————————

I found a great rental online, but they want me to mail the deposit out of the country — is this a scam?

Yes. There are several scams prevalent in today's marketplace. If it sounds too good to be true, it is. Here are some other red flags to look for.

- The property is listed by 2 different parties at 2 different prices on the same website. Or the property is listed on multiple sites at a wide range of prices.

- The price is way below market value.

- The property pops on and off the market within hours.

- The owner of the property is in a foreign country, often saying they are missionaries, military personnel, or professors.

- There is no sign in the yard, or there is a sign and the person is different from who you are talking to online. They will usually tell you not to contact the person on the sign in front of the house, as they have just fired them or something to that effect.

- You are asked to provide personal information — bank account numbers for wiring, social security number, a copy of your driver's license.

- They ask you to just look in the windows, then send or wire money and they will send you the keys.

Be careful and always know who you are dealing with, especially in an online transaction.

How do I protect my property listing from rental scams?

The new big scam I see most often today is a scammer that will lift your property listing information and put it up as a rental. The ads will say something like call me directly, ignore the sign in the yard, or send me $1000 and I'll send you the keys. They are getting more and more sophisticated every day. They will even lookup the owner's name and get an email address with the owner's name in it to answer your inquiry. You feel like you are dealing with the owner, but you are not.

Here is a quick and easy way to check if your property listing has been hijacked as a rental or other listings. Do a web search for your house image. Open 2 windows on your web browser. In one, open an image search tool such as Google Items. Then, in the other, open a website with your listing photo in it. Click on that photo and hold down the mouse button while you drag the picture back into the first window you opened and drop the picture into the search bar. Then you will see all of the places your home photo has been appearing online.

I am looking at my tax roll assessment, is that what my house is really worth?

I have had people who are looking to buy a house pull up the tax roll and tell me the house is only worth so much because that is what the tax roll assessment says. Your tax assessment is what your home is valued at for tax purposes. It does not represent what your home might be worth in today's market.

The tax assessor can only raise the taxes on your homestead a maximum of 2 to 3% a year. So, even if your home may have doubled in value, your assessment will not reflect that. The only time they can fully reassess a home's value is when it is sold. So, if a house has been sold in the last year or two, the tax assessment on the tax roll is probably pretty close to the value of the house if the sale was at market price. But if you have been in your home for more than a couple of years, your tax roll assessment will not be reflective of today's market value at all.

*Tax roll assessments may be viewed at the Florida
Dept. of Revenue - Property Tax - Data Portal*

What is the Save Our Homes Amendment?

The Save Our Homes amendment was brought about because of the inequity in tax roll assessments of a home's value for tax purposes. Someone who has been in their home for quite a long time will have a vastly lower assessment than what their house is worth. So, someone who has just bought a home will get a full tax assessment while the person next door to them may only paying half of that. Some older folks were feeling trapped in their homes because if they moved, they could not afford to pay current tax rates. So the save our home amendment came about, where you could take your lower tax assessment with you to your new home.

So, if your home was assessed $50,000 less than what it was worth today, you would be able to reduce the assessment on your new home by $50,000 in order for you to be able to pay roughly the same in taxes and wouldn't be locked out of moving to a new house because you could not afford the taxes.

Year	Market Value	*Assessed Value	Homestead Exemption	Taxable Value	Taxes With SOH	Taxes Without SOH	Total Savings Due To SOH
1	$110,000	$110,000	$50,000	$60,000	$1,200.00	$1,200.00	$0.00
2	$126,500	$113,300	$50,000	$63,300	$1,266.00	$1,530.00	$264.00
3	$145,475	$116,699	$50,000	$66,699	$1,333.98	$1,909.50	$575.52
4	$167,296	$120,200	$50,000	$70,200	$1,404.00	$2,345.92	$941.92
5	$192,390	$123,806	$50,000	$73,806	$1,476.12	$2,847.80	$1,371.68
*County assessed value						Total Savings	$3,153.12

SOH Example

III
Home Selling To Home Buying, Moving And Miscellaneous

When is the buying season for houses?

People are always asking me if this is a good time to put their homes on the market. Is there a better time than others? There definitely is a cycle when it comes to buying homes. March to June is the high season for buying because everyone wants to move in July — in between school years.

August it slows down quite a bit, as everyone is getting ready for school to start. September to November is a slow but even pace. At the beginning of the holidays, you get the round of investors snapping up properties before the end of the year. That is followed by a steep drop in buyers until the end of the year.

Then on January 1st, we get a surge of calls from new buyers and sellers that lasts for about 2 weeks — about the same as New Year's resolutions.

February is the lowest inventory month because everyone is waiting on the high season to list their homes. So in February, every house sells! Even the ugly ones... Making it a great time to sell.

Is there ever a time or a market when nothing sells?

There has always been a certain amount of houses that sell every single month in Tallahassee. No matter if it is a good or bad market, or the busy or slow time, there are always about 200 houses a month sold here in Tallahassee and the surrounding areas. Because there are always reasons people have to buy and sell houses. There are job transfers, moves, marriages, deaths, divorces, and babies. These things that trigger home sales happen all the time.

What does go up and down is the inventory of homes available for sale. We have an average of around 1200 houses and townhouses on the market at any given time.

When the market was really terrible several years ago, we had 7000 homes on the market. And the 200 sales a month out of 7000 homes available might not seem like much, but houses were still selling at the exact same pace as they always did.

I've bought a house — what type of inspections do I need?

Once you have negotiated a contract on a house, you usually have 10 to 15 days to conduct inspections to verify all of the systems are in good working order. You should start with a full home inspection. These inspectors will check all the systems of the house — the heating & cooling, electrical and plumbing systems as well as any appliances.

Sometimes you will need additional inspections from an expert like an air conditioning company or fireplace specialist if there are any problems found in those areas.

You will also want a radon inspection. Radon is a naturally occurring gas found in the ground that sometimes seeps into homes and causes elevated levels of gas in your house. This can be cured with mitigation, but you will want to test and find out what amount of radon is in your house.

If there is a septic tank, you will need to pay for having the tank pumped as well as the inspection, because they need to pump the tank to be able to visually inspect it. And if there is a pool, you should plan on a pool inspection also.

You should also plan on a WDO (wood destroying organism) or termite inspection to check for woodrot, termites, fungus, mold, carpenter bees, powder post beetles, etc. Quite a lot of inspections, but they will give you some peace of mind.

Depending on the age of your house and roof, your insurance may require a 4 point inspection and a wind mitigation inspection as well.

I am a For Sale By Owner — any advice on showing my home?

Yes, get a realtor! No — just kidding. (kind of...) I do know people who are selling their own homes, and I always give a little safety talk to them with the things that I have learned over the years. First, get all of your buyer's information before you agree to let them into your home. What is their full name, phone number and email address?

Then, when you have them coming to look at your home, have them lead the way. Don't walk into a room first, as they can easily cut off your means of escape. Let them walk into a room first, go up the stairs first, go into the garage or patio first. Always have a direct line to a doorway at all times.

Next, let someone know you are showing the house and feel free to share that information with your buyer. Say "Oh, my sister is coming over when we are done here, she is expecting my call", or something of that nature.

Always remember, no sale is worth your safety.

When a buyer is coming to look at my home, should I be there for the showing?

One of the first questions I usually get on showings is should you be there or not. That is definitely NO. If someone is coming back to look at your home for the 3rd or 4th time, it might not hurt to be around to answer questions, but when they are first coming to look at your home you should not be there.

You may tend to say things that might turn off a potential buyer. I had one seller comment on the deer that would occasionally come into the backyard and how the new buyer was going to have to continue to feed him. The buyer was deathly afraid of animals and immediately crossed that house off her list, even though the house was perfect for her.

I often have For Sale By Owners follow us around and tell us about every project they were intending to do to the house but never got around to. That has no relevance to buyers, they don't care what you were going to do, and they want to think about their own projects and what they want to do. Also, buyers are not comfortable opening your closet doors while you are standing there. And nobody is going to buy a home when they have not looked in the closets. So, as much as you would like to be there to help, it is usually not helpful or a good idea.

What is the difference between 'as-is' compared to 'warranted?'

When you are writing a contract, one of the items to negotiate will be if you are taking the house as is or warranted.

If the seller elects to sell the house warranted, that means the seller is warranting that the systems of the house are in good working order up until the day of closing. Systems are defined as the heating and cooling, electrical, plumbing, and any appliances they are leaving.

If you take the house as is, where is, that means there will be no repairs made at all by the seller. This is often the case with foreclosure sales.

You can also buy a house as-is, but with the seller providing a clear WDO, or wood destroying organism report, also known as the termite letter. Some banks will require a clear WDO for your mortgage. This means the seller will fix anything that will destroy wood, defined as woodrot, fungus, mold, carpenter bees, powder post beetles, or termites.

You also usually get a certain time period to do inspections (anywhere between 7 to 14 days) and you can back out if you don't like the inspection results.

So, purchasing a house as is can mean 2 different things. Negotiate accordingly.

What is the difference between a warranted home and a home warranty?

Many people confuse a warranted home with a home warranty. When you buy a house, you can buy it as is, or warranted. Warranted means the seller would fix anything found wrong with the systems of the house. The heating and air, the plumbing system, the electrical system and any appliances they leave. You can also buy a house with or without a clear WDO or termite letter, but that is a different part. That covers woodrot, fungus, mold, carpenter bees, and things like that. But warranted means the seller is warranting the systems of the house to be in working order until the day of closing.

A home warranty is basically an insurance policy you can buy to cover the systems of the house. They are usually for one year and cost somewhere between $400 to $700 depending on how many add-on's you want. If anything goes wrong with any of your systems or appliances, you call the warranty company, and for a standard fee, usually $75 or $100 they will come out and fix or replace the item that is broken. If they are replacing an item, there are usually a few pieces and parts or wires or tubes they won't cover, so you may have some additional charges

I am moving — do I have to move everything?

If you are moving, this is a great time to go through your belongings, get rid of some stuff and simplify your life a little bit. There are many wonderful charities that you can donate quite a variety of items to and some of them will even pick up.

Think of the items you have been debating letting go of and donate some of that furniture, trim down your kitchen gadgets and appliances, and go through your clothes and donate anything you haven't worn in the last 2 years.

Clean out your entire pantry and take everything that is not expired to a local food bank and feed some of the hungry folks around town. Don't forget to grab a receipt and give it to your accountant at the end of the year for a tax deduction.

Donating is a great way to free up some space, help the local community, trim down the number of boxes that you will have to move and get a tax deduction. What a smart way to save some money on your move.

Donating is a great way to free up some space.

What are some good tips for moving?

Moving is always a little crazy, so the following tips and tricks may help with the havoc.

When packing glasses, put them in socks to help prevent cracks. Also, you can usually pick up boxes with cardboard separators at your local liquor store. When you are packing your ceramic plates, use bubble wrap or put paper plates in between them.

To prevent necklaces and bracelets from tangling up, use an empty toilet paper roll or a drinking straw. Thread each chain through the toilet paper roll or the straw and fasten the clasp.

Slide a trash bag over your hanging clothes to make them easier to stack and carry. Use your towels, sheets, and dishcloths to cushion other objects. Pack pillows at the top of your boxes, and wrap artwork in blankets.

For electronics — use the plastic tabs from bread to wrap electronic cords and prevent tangles. Be sure to label them, and snap a picture of where they were before you disconnect them to make it easier to reconnect them in your new home.

Do you have any ideas to make moving easier?

Moving is never easy, but here are a few tips to help with the headache of moving into your new home.

Photograph all of your cords. This will make it easier to reconnect them later.

Get a movers guide from the post office. You need to notify them of your new address anyways, and it includes helpful coupons.

Color-code your boxes to the different rooms in the house.

Anything you need immediately after move-in should be marked in red or put in a red box. Make sure the red boxes go on the truck last, so they will come off the truck first.

Your red boxes should contain one first night essential box. Put in medications, toothbrushes change of clothes, anything else you need that first night.

Pack a first-day cleaning kit so you can clean out cabinets and closets before you move your items in.

And, put your valuables, purse and important documents in a special box, and put that in your car and lock it, away from all the moving activity.

How can I find a good repair guy?

Realtors are a great resource for all sorts of information in the community. Don't be afraid to use them! Realtors are not just for buying and selling houses. We all have a trusted list of vendors and service people that we use and every one of us would be happy to share those recommendations with you — as well as provide you with the names and phone numbers.

Feel free to call if you are looking for ceramic tile guys, carpenters, and plumbers. If you are putting on an addition to your house, need a tree removed or pruned, need a couch, need to sell a couch, or if you are looking for maid service, a pressure washer, window washer, or dog walker, we know hundreds of people. Think of us as a mini Angie's list.

Local Realtors know about the city and the surrounding areas also. Looking for something to do or have relatives in town? Call us about trails, parks, beaches, culture and arts, the Tallahassee

Museum, Wakulla Springs, the 22nd floor of the capital, and local and regional attractions and points of interest. Realtors are a wealth of knowledge. Feel free to call one today!

How do I become a real estate agent?

This is a question I do get quite often. If you are thinking about starting a career in Real Estate, I would suggest having 6 months of savings in the bank. This gives you plenty of time to get started and established without having to panic about paying the next month's bills.

Look into taking a class to prepare you for the test. You can do this locally in a sit-down classroom, or take a class online. Then you need to take and pass the Real Estate Test. Then start interviewing real estate companies and ask about their training programs. You can also get training at the Board of Realtors.

And, speaking of the Board, you should join the Tallahassee Board of Realtors, as well as the Florida Association of Realtors, and the National Board of Realtors. Buy some business cards to start passing out. You will need to apply for your realtor key. You can expect to spend at least $1000 on the expenses just listed to get started in the business. If you have the energy and are organized, real estate could be a great career for you!

What is the oldest building in Tallahassee?

The oldest building in Tallahassee is known as The Columns and was built by William Money Williams in 1830. It was originally on Park Ave and Adams Street but was moved to 100 N. Duval Street in 1971. It is now home to the James Madison Institute.

And here are some other fun facts about Tallahassee:

- The current capitol building, designed by Edward Stone, is the 3rd tallest capitol building in the United States, right after Washington DC and Austin.

- The Tallahassee police department is the 3rd oldest in the nation. Founded in 1841, only Philadelphia and Boston police departments predate it.

- Doak Campbell Stadium is the biggest

Atlantic Coast Conference football stadium and is also the country's largest continuous brick structure.

- Also, FSU is believed to be where streaking was invented.

- Wally Amos, founder of Famous Amos Cookies was born and raised in Tallahassee.

- Union forces captured every confederate state capital city east of the Mississippi River except for one during the civil war. That city was Tallahassee.

- Tallahassee is the only Florida city that has recorded a subzero temperature. It was -2 degrees in February 1899.

Conclusion

Thank you so much for reading, or flipping through *Real Advice from the Real Estate Advisors.* I hope you found something helpful you can put to use today.

Do you have a question you would like answered on the air? Need service or repair people? Need some free advice? Or, if you would just like to hear some fast, funny and fascinating real estate stories, give me a call.

Real Estate is a very interesting business! I have seen just about everything, so I may have some great advice for your particular situation. If I don't know the answer, I know the person who does.

Cindy Cooper
Cindy@TLHRealtors.com 850-545-8076

I know many good resource people who are knowledgeable and always willing to help.

Feel free to call, text or email. I may be reached at:

Cindy Cooper <u>Cindy@TLHRealtors.com</u>
850-545-8076

To listen to these shows or glean more advice from the Real Estate advisors, visit our website at
<u>www.TLHRealtors.com</u>

And always remember — I have a key to every house in town!

Made in the USA
Columbia, SC
17 February 2023

12438188R00063